Wonders of America

Niagara Falls

For Brannon, at last!—M. D. B.

To T. J., Jackson, and Aidan—J. W.

SIMON SPOTLIGHT
An imprint of Simon & Schuster Children's Publishing Division
1230 Avenue of the Americas, New York, NY 10020
This Simon Spotlight edition August 2019
First Aladdin Paperbacks edition June 2006
Text copyright © 2006 by Marion Dane Bauer
Illustrations copyright © 2006 by John Wallace
All rights reserved, including the right of reproduction
in whole or in part in any form.
SIMON SPOTLIGHT, READY-TO-READ, and colophon are registered
trademarks of Simon & Schuster, Inc.
For information about special discounts for bulk purchases, please
contact Simon & Schuster Special Sales at 1-866-506-1949 or
business@simonandschuster.com.
Manufactured in the United States of America 0719 LAK
2 4 6 8 10 9 7 5 3 1
Library of Congress Cataloging-in-Publication Data
Bauer, Marion Dane.
Niagara Falls / by Marion Dane Bauer ; illustrated by
John Wallace.— 1st Aladdin Paperbacks ed.
p. cm.—(Ready-to-read) (Wonders of America)
1. Niagara Falls (N.Y. and Ont.)—Juvenile literature.
I. Wallace, John, 1966– ill. II. Title. III. Series.
F127.N8B35 2006   971.3'39—dc22   2005017586
ISBN 978-1-5344-4540-6 (hc)
ISBN 978-0-689-86944-0 (pbk)

Wonders of America

Niagara Falls

By **Marion Dane Bauer**

Illustrated by **John Wallace**

Ready-to-Read

SIMON SPOTLIGHT

New York London Toronto Sydney New Delhi

It all began with ice.

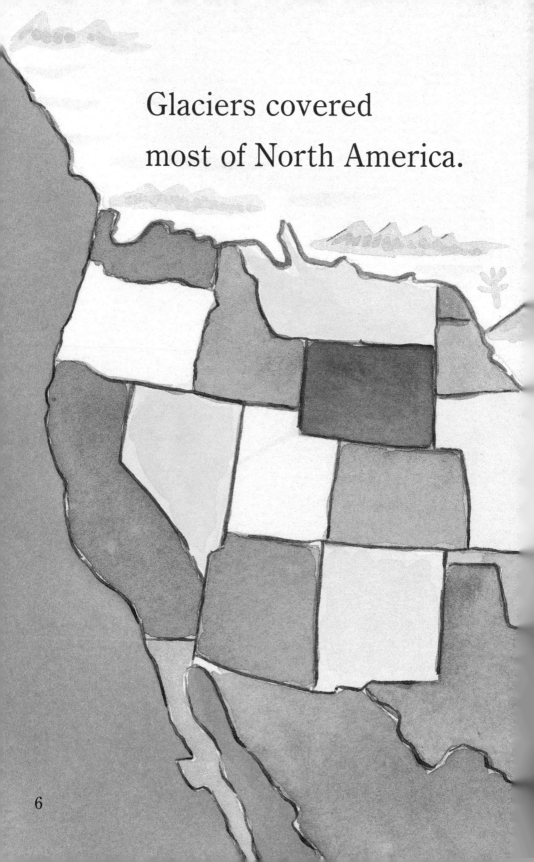

Glaciers covered
most of North America.

A glacier (glay-shur)
is ice made from old snow.
The snow has been packed
down for many, many years.

This ice moved
across the land.
It scooped out holes.

Lake Superior

Lake

Lake Michigan

Chicago •

Detroit •

When the glaciers melted,
they left lakes
and rivers behind.
They formed the Great Lakes.

Huron

Toronto •

Lake Ontario

• Niagara

Lake Erie

They formed Niagara Falls.
"Niagara" comes from
a Seneca Indian word.

It means "thunder of
the waters."
And the waters do thunder.
Every second, 400,000 gallons
go over the Falls.

Niagara Falls
was North America's
first tourist attraction.

One part of the Falls,
the Horseshoe Falls,
is in Canada.

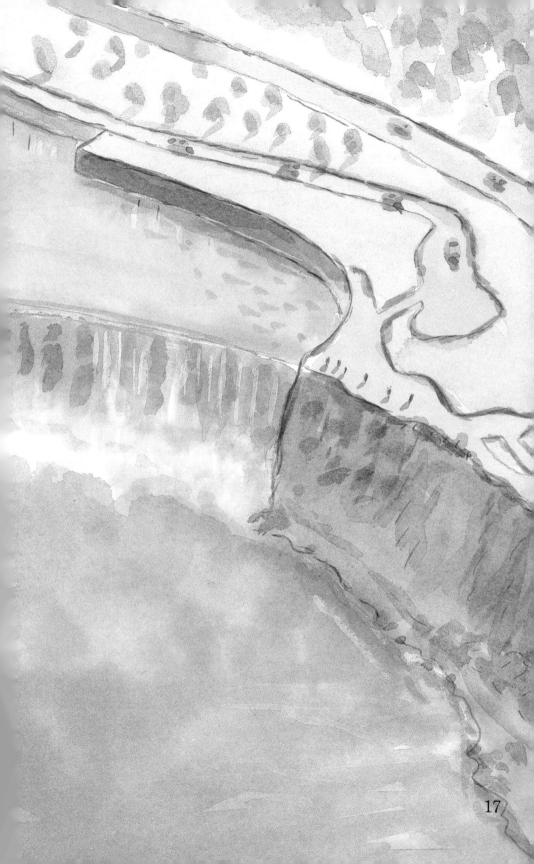

The other part is
in the United States.

Horseshoe
Falls

Bridal Veil
Falls

The Falls turn some people
into daredevils.

Annie Taylor,
a 63-year-old teacher,
was the first
to go over the Falls
in a barrel.

She said afterward,
"No one ought ever
do that again."

But many people have.
Some have died doing it.

A man named Blondin
walked a tightrope
across the Falls.
He carried his manager.

Now there are laws
against such stunts.

But we do not need stunts
to find the Falls exciting
and beautiful.

They are both!

Interesting Facts about Niagara Falls

★ More than twelve million people come to see the Niagara Falls every year. It is a popular place for couples to visit on their honeymoons.

★ An ice bridge sometimes forms at the base of the Falls in winter. People used to walk out onto it. They even set up stands on the ice and sold souvenirs. One day a chunk of ice broke free, and three people were drowned in the whirlpool below.

★ Power plants on both sides of the Niagara River use the force of the water to produce electricity. They produce billions of kilowatt-hours of electricity every year.

★ Many people have made money from the tourists coming to Niagara Falls. Some even sold "petrified mist." The "mist" was really ordinary stones imported from England.

★ In 1678, Father Louis Hennepin was the first European to see the Falls and write about what he saw. However, he was so impressed that he said the Falls were more than 500 feet tall. They are actually about 190 feet tall.

★ The Falls are over 12,000 years old. In that time they have created a gorge seven miles long.